Love Your Business, Love Your Life

By: Ellicia Romo

Table of Contents

Introduction 9

Broken Dreams 13

Big Changes 21

Eight Touch System 31

How Does It Happen? What to Do Now! 37

Everyone Knows What I Do 45

How to Build Relationships 51

How Do I Connect? 59

Referral Partners Are Our Friends! 67

Finding Your Partners 71

Collaboration VS Competition 77

Build the Relationship, But Don't Get Burned! 85

Exchange of Value 91

Getting and Keeping Loyal Partners 97

Let's Connect 101

Introduction

Are you a people person? I love people. I've always liked people. You probably have friends and loved ones. I bet those friends are an important part of your life. You also value your family and the relationships around you. You may have come to a conclusion that happy people have great relationships with others. People may not always remember the tasks that you have completed or the stuff you have owned, but they will remember how they felt when they were around you. A huge part of going to work is building relationships with the people you interact with and finding ways to meet their needs, as well as getting your own needs met. This doesn't matter if it is a coworker or a client; a boss or a subordinate. I've learned to be good at bringing people into my circle and helping them; and I have found that when it comes to business, it is sometimes difficult without the proper foundation being laid first. In business, sustainability, consistency, and growth is really the goal-- and sometimes you find yourself feeling like it's more of a roller coaster ride. The good news is: You CAN create that sustainability, consistency, and continued growth. You don't need to be on a roller coaster of emotions or income. And it can be fun!

Imagine how it would feel if every day you had a plan of how to meet people—not just random people, not just people you wish you were working with—but rather, the right kind of people that you love getting up and going to work with and working for, so that "work" can become "fun" and with the foundation of relationships already built, you can press on to the sustainability that you're looking for.

I know through my own experience that if you build your business through building your relationships, you will have that solid, sustainable business. You may ride rolling hills, rather than roller coasters. Plus, it's more fun to work with friends, rather than strangers! My programs, workshops, and/or coaching will show you proven methods of how to make that happen. In this book, we are focusing on building relationships because it is the key to the foundation of that solid sustainable business. Are you ready for the change? Are you ready to have a steady income?

What I found in life is that I don't want to work with people or do business with people (or their company) that I wouldn't want to be friends with. I have grown both my personal life and my business after I learned the principles of only creating relationships that are mutually successful, and then applying those principles in business to grow my income, as well. Let's face it, working with people that you don't ever want to see or hear from after work hours is not fun or enjoyable in any way. Those are the times that you count down to the weekends, or dread upcoming Mondays. What if you never dreaded another Monday again? Would your life, not just your work life, but the quality of your overall life, be better? Would you be happier? Would you maybe treat others around you better and raise the quality of your relationships?

I've learned the lessons the hard way, and I'm sharing those lessons to make it easier for you to find the same success. You can work with people that you enjoy and respect, and you can increase your income while boosting your success in business. I know, because I did it. Stick with me through this short book. Then later, join me in one of my business coaching programs, where I will give you more tips for you to follow, on your way to building your foundation for personal and professional success.

My mission in life is to touch hundreds of thousands of lives, to support people in their growth, and to inspire people and help them transform their business, their income, self- esteem; and overall grow their lives to be the best they can be. My own journey is one of rags-to-riches, in a way. After a divorce, and while being a single mom, I had absolutely nothing. I spent my time looking for ways to make more money. I had yard sales every weekend just trying to make ends meet. I searched Craigslist for odd jobs and jumped at the chance of some quick money. More than anything, I wanted to find a better way of life, so that I could properly support my son. I had to find a way. I would not be dependent on anyone else for money. I was determined to make it. To rise above. To be the example. To prove it could be done. I set a goal to be in a place where I didn't feel the need to tell my son "no" because we could not afford it. If I said no to something, it would be because I truly didn't want to spend the money, not because I didn't have the money. Here is how my story goes:

Chapter One

Broken Dreams

As a young person, I hated school, I dreaded going, I was labeled the problem child who talked too much and wouldn't obey the rules; but at the age of 7, I met the woman who made the difference I needed. Who made me feel important, who included me in what was happening, rather than attempt to control my actions and expect me to just be quiet. The woman who cared about me, my opinions, and what I wanted and needed. The woman who made a difference to every child in her classroom, because she allowed them to feel that they made a difference to her. She had a way of making her students feel important. I spent most of my childhood wanting to be just like my second grade teacher, Mrs. Hegline. I wanted to emulate her and walk in her footsteps. I wanted to make a difference. I wanted people to want to be around me. I wanted the respect that I saw her receive, even by the "problem kids" because she was making a difference in our lives, and we knew it. We knew she cared about us. She was unlike any other teacher in my elementary school. I loved to be around her so much, I spent many days staying after school to "help her." All the while, I am now sure, she was helping me.

Ten years later, still with a dream to be like Mrs. Hegline, I went to college and graduated with a degree in elementary education. I began my teaching career in a small town in northern AZ, teaching 6th grade. I married a local man, who was in the banking industry and just getting his start in business. While we got by, we both realized we were not on the path to fully realize our individual professional capabilities. After many nights of tears and days of frustration, I concluded that the Arizona public school system was not where I was meant to spend the rest of my adult life. The politics in the school systems made it to where I felt that I could not make the impact I knew that I was put on this earth to accomplish. It seemed that the parents who were well connected, donated money, or were influencers in the community got what they wanted for their kids, no matter if it was for the good or not so good of the mass of the student body. Decisions were being made that were not in alignment with what I felt was the best for the students that I was teaching. Test scores were also more important than the actual learning and progress of the students. I was not making the impact that I wanted to make, and I knew I was capable of making a bigger impact. I felt like a failure. I was no Mrs. Hegline. I did not create the atmosphere in my classroom that I strived to create. I knew there had to be another way. I also needed to achieve financial security for my family, now with a new infant, and could not figure out how to do that, while impacting children in the Arizona public schools.

In searching for a solution to my frustration and failure, I decided I needed something new to do. I made the decision to go back to school. I was taught to go to school, get a good education, and then, get a good job with a pension. Let's face it, this is what I felt was the societal norm, and I definitely wanted to be "normal". When the good job wasn't working for me, all I knew (or thought I knew) to make a change, was to get more of a formal education. I asked myself, "With a Bachelor's degree in education, what can I get a Master's in?" My logical answer was... education. So, off I went!

I knew I didn't really want to be in education, anymore. Although, I was stuck (at least, I thought so). I knew of no way out, and options were limited. I was frustrated. I had even applied at fast food restaurants and was told I was overqualified for the $7 an hour starting position and underqualified for the manager's position. Halfway through a dual masters in elementary education and school counseling, the changes I was looking for appeared before me. I found my way out! I found a new path to travel. A new way to impact others, while continuing my own growth.

Do you believe in fate? How about the Law of Attraction? The Law of Attraction is a universal law that creates results in life. Everything is created twice; first in thought, then in material results. What you put your focus on, what you believe you can have and are worthy of, you can create. It deals with the power of thought and the power of the human mind. I learned a lot about this when I started reading books on success like, Think and Grow Rich by Napoleon Hill, The Secret by Rhonda Byrne, and Law of Attraction by Michael Losier.

I believe that everything happens for a reason. What you think about, you bring about; and what you focus on grows, and boy, was I focused on getting out of the public school system! What I focused on, I brought into my life. I didn't know how, I just knew I had to find a new path. Maybe "normal" wasn't for me, anymore. As Ralph Waldo Emerson once said, "Once you make a decision, the universe conspires to make it happen."

And happen it did... Imagine it, the room was hot, crowded, smelled of food, sweat and farm animals. It was extremely noisy. There were people everywhere. Rows and aisles of vendors. As crazy as it sounds, my new opportunity came while I was visiting the Arizona State Fair. In the middle of all the activity, I saw a tall clear glass box with money flying around inside. I was drawn to the display box where that money was blowing and swirling. I wanted more money in my life, so naturally, that caught my attention. I was walking through an aisle at the state fair vendor expo. The man behind the table said, "Take a guess on how much money is inside, and win it all!" I wrote my guess on the entry slip. There it was at the bottom of the entry slip, my golden ticket, "Are you interested in a career change?" Of course, I marked YES!

A few days later, I received the call. The caller asked me if I would be interested in a new career. My heart was pounding, and the caller outlined the possibilities and asked if I would like to schedule a meeting to discuss this opportunity further. Again, of course, I said "yes" and proceeded to schedule a meeting to discuss a career change opportunity further. Soon, on the appointed date (it was a Tuesday evening), I walked into the meeting. My palms were sweaty, and my heart raced, as I walked into the room to learn about this new career opportunity. Could this be my way out of my financial rut and on to a path of financial independence? Could this be the change I needed to not feel like a failure anymore?

Indeed, it was! I accepted the position in financial sales, selling life and health insurance with a company called Primerica Financial Services (PFS). Selling mutual fund investments and training new sales representatives would shortly follow. I had intense training sessions on sales, products, and understanding personality styles. I studied hard, went to the company's insurance school, took the tests, and earned my life and health insurance licenses along with a series 6 and 63 (which are the uniform securities agents licenses needed to sell securities, mutual funds and retirement account investments) in order to sell mutual fund investments and set up retirement accounts. I was finally on my way. They allowed me to start part-time, and I had a plan to work my way out of the public-school system. I was on my way to replace my measly income and make considerably more than the typical salary an Arizona public school teacher made at the time.

I listened, I learned, I practiced my scripts, I trained, and became a great follower; because I believe that great followers make great leaders. I learned about people's personality types; so I could work with everyone in a more effective manner. I learned how to close sales. I asked a lot of questions, both; to understand my craft and my client's needs, and to close business. I learned to guide conversations, and I got the sales. I quickly rose to the top in sales, in my office. I was getting recognized at big events and started speaking from the stage. I began training others, so this put my teaching skills back to use. At the same time, I rode the sales person's roller coaster. The ups and downs in income, and the ups and downs of emotions that went along with that. Month after month, day after day, feeling like I was continuously starting over. Always looking for that next sale, the next prospect. I didn't really know what referral business looked like or felt like.

I watched and listened to training from the company bigwigs, from around the country. I kept hearing about building relationships and asking for referral business. I thought I was doing that. I thought I understood. I would ask for referrals and didn't often get any. I obviously didn't embody the concept of building relationships. People trusted me to be their agent. However, it seemed they didn't trust me enough to let me sit down with their friends and family. My local mentors taught me about closing sales. I was clearly focused on that. I closed sales well, but that didn't make everything in my life perfect. Not personally, or professionally. I was still finding myself in the struggle. Unfulfilled and living paycheck to paycheck.

Chapter Two
Big Changes

Leaving my workday, I would come home to a bigger roller coaster of emotions. There was yelling and tears, when I walked through the door. My marriage was deteriorating, and the stress of the business did not make it any easier. Our marriage was destructive, dysfunctional, and abusive. My husband, who was also experiencing his own career frustrations, would often ask me when I was going to get a "real job" because he didn't think that commission work was real work. He valued my teaching job and the steady pay over the potential of commission sales. It was a sense of status for him to be married to a teacher when we were in the small town he grew up in; but we moved to the Phoenix area, and we both became smaller fish in a big ocean. I felt like my life was miserable and crumbling, at the time. My husband lost his job at the bank and actually chose to come work at Primerica, with me. We were going to be a team. I knew this would make or break the relationship. We could work together toward a common good, or our deficiencies would be brought to a bigger/brighter light. It's not surprising that our personal and professional lives became worse, with us. The arguments grew stronger, and the fights were louder and more hurtful. Once I saw my son begin to treat other people the way that my ex and I treated each other, I knew I had to do something. I knew that in staying together as a couple, we were creating a poor example for our son. We were not teaching him healthy ways of coping with people or problems.

I knew if my life was to change, I had to change. I gathered up the strength to file for divorce, and began to do personal growth and spiritual work. Since my ex and I worked together and lived together, I also chose to leave the world of insurance and investments. Breaking completely free was a great idea and very important to me. However, it was an extremely scary choice because now I was left with nothing. I was living on food stamps and scrounging to make it. I had to find a way to support myself and my son, and that was the top priority; but I knew I wanted to do it on my own. I had to do it on my own. No one could do it for me. I wanted to be the example for my son to see that we can get through anything and create a life that we design. If I could have success, he would have the example he needed. If I could do it, he could see that he could do it, too. Now, it was time to prove what my mother told me when I was a child, "You can do anything you set your mind to".

If you have ever been through a divorce, you know that friendships also change. Many relationships, not just the romantic and family ones, change or leave your life for good. I needed new friends if I was going to survive this divorce. I needed new friends, fast. A divorce is usually a tough time and can be even tougher if you are going through it alone. I was already on a mission to create a new life—I thought I might as well do it right!

The divorce gave me the motivation I needed to take care of us (my son and I) on my own. I was determined to do this without needing money from my ex, and I wanted to be a great example for my son; so I found a new way to bring in money and become financially independent. While going through the divorce, my ex and I were still living together; and working together was no longer an option. I knew I had to change that, so I entered the world of real estate. I started with delivering The Real Estate Book as a side job which I had found on Craigslist. This was a magazine that was free to the public, filled with real estate ads. It was published and delivered to stands and businesses once a month. The job was a way to get out of the financial services office I was working in. While serving as delivery person, a sales position opened up, and I jumped at it. I had to prove to the boss I could sell. He saw me as only a delivery driver. Using my powers of persuasion, I talked him into giving me a shot, on a trial basis. I sold ads to Realtors and loan originators for The Real Estate Book for over a year. Starting with one territory/book and growing to cover three territories/books. It was low pay and a lot of work. I knew I wasn't going to get financially independent staying there. Although I was grateful for the transition opportunity. I searched and found a new job with a small title service agency. This position was offered to me, in part, because of the relationships

I made in selling advertising in The Real Estate Book. They weren't ready to hire for the role yet. I was connected to the general manager from one of their current employees that I had met earlier in the year at a networking event. When I mentioned how big my database of Realtors was, the manager stopped telling me there was nothing available and set up an interview time. My connections, my list, my database (my industry relationships and friendships) made me look valuable enough to the company that the door opened enough for the interview. Now, it was up to me to sell myself and get hired.

I was successful as a Title and Escrow company's sales and marketing representative. I had a great mentor within the company, and strove to top all goals and challenges, I created out-of-the-box marketing opportunities, worked relentlessly, and achieved success within the company. I continued to deepen my relationships that I built from The Real Estate Book and grew lots of new ones. The company gave me the opportunity to attend new networking events, where I made many new connections. I still wanted more, though. Now, armed with an even more complete list of contacts within the real estate industry, and a growing reputation as a tireless worker and novel marketer, I landed a position as the Director of Marketing and Business Development for a national mortgage company, based locally, in Arizona. At first, I was bringing in business to the company and to individual loan originators. Then, I started thinking about the fact that I, as one person, could only do so much. I thought about all that I had learned about leverage and realized it was time to leverage the 100 loan originators that I was working with. I began to teach and mentor the loan originators and the Realtors that work with them about building business through building relationships. Much of my job became teaching them to do what I had learned to do. It was a no-brainer, win-win solution. Teach the Realtors to grow their business, and teach the loan originators to build and maintain the relationships with both the Realtors and their past buyers; and the referrals would come. Realtors made more money, loan originators made more money, the company grew, and in turn, my income grew. We all won.

After 7 years as the Director of Marketing and Business Development, I decided to put myself back into sales and use what has worked for me in the past again. I am having fun doing what I have taught others to do and having success from the ground up one more time. I was a beginner again. I went to school to become a mortgage loan originator, studied, took the exam and got my license. I made a move to the largest mortgage broker in the country, NEXA Mortgage. I started at the bottom one more time. Within 3 months I was doing what takes the average new loan originator 6-12 months to accomplish. I was just doing what I preached to others in the past. I worked through my relationships and worked 100% by referral. Two plus years have now passed, and I have stayed working 100% by referral and I have been able to have my income consistently grow and have not had to ride the roller coaster of income and emotions. I plan to continue to grow, teach, mentor and train and have fun doing it. The fun comes because I get to work with great people that I care about and love. I get recruit and mentor loan originators from all walks of life and all over the country. I get to build more relationships and make the difference I know I can make. I can do it all at NEXA Mortgage.

Why did I originally choose NEXA Mortgage, you might ask. It was because of the very reasons that I discuss throughout this book. Ten years before I made the move, I met Mike Kortas. I was working for The Real Estate Book and he was working as a branch manager and mortgage loan originator. We connected and realized that we had similar success goals and we both needed to meet more Realtors. Mike saw that I had the ability to network, connect and gain the trust of local Realtors. I saw his drive, his grit, determination, and a great program that Realtors would want. Mike was honest, transparent, and real. I knew I could work with him and I quickly considered him a friend. We both saw the value in a potential business collaboration. We started hosting classes and event together and both invited our sphere of Realtors. That continued while I worked in the title and escrow industry. However, when I moved into the mortgage space we became somewhat of a competitor to each other. I believe in building relationships and not burning bridges. We live in a small world and you never know when times and people will circle back in your life in a way that you might need or want them. During my tenure at the other mortgage company, Mike and I stayed in contact. We remained friends and checked in on each other from time to time. Of course, we each worked on recruiting the other so that we could work together again. In the end, Mike won. Actually we both won. Mike never found a mortgage company that he was 100% happy at, so he started NEXA Mortgage, LLC. When it was time for me to make a change, I knew joining Mike's company was the best place for me. In part because it's a great company and has an amazing structure. However, the bigger part was because of my relationship with Mike. I knew I could trust him, I knew he had the backs of everyone in the company and I knew if he said it, it was true and he believed it. It was the know, like and trust factor you will hear me mention throughout this book. At this time, I am extremely happy to be at NEXA and glad that Mike had developed the business relationship that we did, or I would not be where I am today.

Early into my real estate career, I discovered networking events. I discovered it to be my new way to make friends that worked in the real estate industry. The world was changing; and not many people in the industry, in Arizona, worked in an office anymore. The way to meet people was not dropping into an office, because the offices were bare. I truly began to discover the meaning of building business through building relationships. I made new friends, out of necessity for my personal life and to get my foot in the door with more Realtors and loan originators. As my friendships grew, so did my business. When I was selling ads for The Real Estate Book, I had early success in the real estate industry, and I found the transition from insurance and investments to real estate advertisement sales to be an easy one. I knew how to close. Now, I was making friends and my friends wanted to do business with me. How great is that? I quickly learned that when you are selling something to people, especially when it's a service, it doesn't really matter what you are selling. What matters is how you work with the people, how you treat people, and how you build relationships. These relationships built in a positive manner will create repeat and referral business. When people like you and like the service you provide, they will tell their friends. They will also work with you again, and again. It's the age old saying that people will work with people that they know, like, and trust. I recently had a friend recommend a restaurant to me, and she said when I get there, I should ask for Humberto. Humberto was her favorite waiter. Did she recommend I go there because of the business name or the company, or did she recommend I go and ask for Humberto because she liked, trusted, and respected him? It's the same thing in any business. People work with people. They won't work with you, just because of the company you work for or with. They will work with you and hire you for your services, because of who you are and how you treat them. If you work for a company they say they already like, I bet it's because of how someone before you treated them.

Chapter Three

Eight Touch System

I created a system to follow up with people that I met from the networking events I attended. I call it my 8 touch system. It requires 8 touches in 14 days. That's the start of building those friendships and relationships. When you see someone as a transaction you might not want to connect every day for a week or two, however would you want to connect with a friend every day? Most people don't worry too much about reaching out to a friend. Start seeing new clients as friends, and you won't worry about "bugging" them, because you won't be. Those 8 touches aren't about asking for a sale. They are truly about building the relationship. It can be a social media connection, or a text, a private message or a nice-to-meet-you card or even a short video message. I ask for the business when we sit down face to face for coffee or lunch, after taking time to get to know the person, first. Of course, it's also after I have decided I want to work with them. Just like I learned that people will want to work with me, if they know, like, and trust me, I also only want to work with them if I feel like I know, like, and trust them. It may take some time to get to that point, and it may happen quickly, there are many factors that can determine the time frame. However, it can't be forced. Each person must be genuine in their interaction with the other. This statement shows that I also learned I must let my true self shine. No longer would I be the person I thought they wanted me to be. I was going to be true to me. That way, the relationships being built are genuine and will not fall apart if/when the "true me" came out.

Transactions VS Relations

After finding some success and making another one of my growth transitions, from sales representative of The Real Estate Book to a title and escrow company account executive, to a Director of Marketing and Business Development; I came to realize that in the world of insurance and investments, I was working transactionally. Meaning; going from one transaction to another. Always looking for the next deal. Not doing great follow up and staying in touch with clients after the deal closed. One deal would close, and I was immediately on to the next one. I knew I needed to be relational, and I thought I was. I thought being friendly in appointments and feeling like they were friendly, back, was enough. However, until I needed to make new friends, I didn't really see and know the difference. In my mind, I knew I was to work on relationships. However, my mind and my actions were clearly out of sync. Not many of my insurance clients were true friends. There is a difference between transactional approach and relational approach in business. A lot of people in sales and service-related industries have the transactional approach; and those people ride a constant roller coaster of income, success, and emotions. A transactional approach focuses on closing the deal and hurrying on to the next one; whereas with the relational approach, you focus on building a relationship with the prospective client and past clients. Transactional approaches leave you starting over and seeking the next paycheck. When you've closed with a client, it's almost like being unemployed after each commission check. You feel employed when you have a deal going and almost feel unemployed when you don't. Like seeking the next job over, and over again. Which is why it is a roller coaster of income and emotions. Searching for each new client is like a job hunt. The relational approach creates multiple advocates for you; which turns into having ambassadors in your corner, as well as a great group of new friends. Relationships are emotional and result in you getting to enjoy the compounding effect (this is the ability of an asset to generate earnings which then are reinvested to generate their own earnings) of your efforts and friendships. The obvious choice is to build that Know Like and Trust factor and create friendships first. It's a choice between the roller coaster of starting over, and over; or compounding referrals, recommendations, and friends in your life. Business can come to you, or you can chase after the business. Friends want to help you grow and will support you along the way, especially if you ask for the support you need. When they know you want referrals and connections, they will most likely offer them to you.

You may just have to teach them how to do it and remind them periodically, and they will be there for you; because friends like to help friends. The choice is yours: be relational and create a sustainable business with great people all around you, or be transactional and live the day-to-day grind.

Supporting my belief that relationships is what makes business strong, continuously growing, and sustainable was the award I received. After a few short years in the industry, I was awarded recognition as a "Woman of Strength" at the Women of Strength event, hosted and founded by Suzy Levenda; and usually held in Scottsdale, AZ. The event sells out two times a year with 400 - 500 hundred people in the real estate industry in the Phoenix area. I was awarded this recognition in part for my ability to create meaningful relationships quickly and for making a difference to those people in their business and personal lives. This was, and is, still is a huge honor. Wearing the necklace that is given as the award to the recipients reminds me each day to continue to build my relationships and make a difference. When people's careers or lives end, do you think they get talked about for the amount of deals they closed, or do they get talked about for their relationships, how they treated people, and how they made a difference? Do people show up to a funeral, just because they were a client, or might a client show up because they were also a friend? You know these answers. It's about the person-to-person connection. Have you thought about the legacy you are leaving and what people will say about you, when you are no longer here?

Now, at this point in my life, I am on a mission. My mission is to make a difference to hundreds of thousands of people, by empowering them to grow their business and hit the goals that they are dreaming of. I am teaching and coaching others who no longer want to struggle with the roller coaster of income and the roller coaster of emotions that comes with sales positions, especially those that are selling their services. I want everyone to know that they no longer have to struggle. If this is you, know that money can come easily if you let it and believe it to be so. Business can grow and be sustainable, and you do not have to have the low lows that come after the high highs. Plus, it can be fun and rewarding. I know it's possible, no matter what your goals are. As it's been said by many before me, "If you can believe it, you can achieve it."

Chapter Four

How Does It Happen? What to Do Now!

Let's talk about that roller-coaster I mentioned earlier. It's the cycle that no one wants to be on, but everyone seems to get on. You work hard marketing yourself and prospecting, you get some deals in the pipeline, and then some deals close. It may be your best month ever. Then, you realize that while you were working on converting what's in your pipeline and closing what you've converted, you forgot to keep marketing and prospecting. Now, you have nothing in the pipeline. You are essentially unemployed, all over again, and starting from scratch. The problem occurs, when you make this roller coaster your habit.

You may even have a great month and then take a vacation. Not having the systems in place that will keep you marketing in your absence adds to the roller coaster effect. When you come home, you again have an empty pipeline, and you are starting over.

The process of keeping business rolling is actually simple with a system of consistency, referral partnerships, and former clients who love the service you provide. Most people don't succeed because they lack the consistency and/or they forget to ever leverage others or create automation in their marketing.

If you look at each transaction as just that-- a transaction-- when you close the deal, you have to go find the next transaction. When you look at each transaction as building friendships, fans, and a volunteer sales force; you can create leverage. Business will eventually be coming to you, without you having to always go out and look for it. You will create leverage and a consistent flow of income. Your business will continue to grow and will be a long-term sustainable source of income; and maybe even freedom, if you allow it to be.

Which would you prefer: to close a deal and start over, and start over, and start over again; or to close a deal, grow your friendships, grow your income, get referrals, and have a sustainable flow of leads? If you chose option two, keep reading.

Are you a serious, all-business type of person, or are you the type of person who likes to have fun and be around friends and family? What if you could be both? We will also go over how you can build your business through building friendships, while at the same time, being highly regarded as a business professional. It's time to start seeing clients as friends, and not just another client. It's also time to see friends and family as clients. The two do not have to be separated. They can all be one and the same. Some people see clients as a dollar sign or a paycheck. If you do that, they know it. They can feel and sense your motives. You may close the transaction; however, most people don't care about how much you know until they know how much you care. In the same sense, they may be happy you helped them get what they want, you closed the deal, and hopefully created a win/win situation. They will walk away satisfied. What if through the transaction they felt a deep sense of caring from you? What if they knew that every time you asked them to decide on something, you were working to help them make a decision that was best for them, regardless of how much money you will make? Now, they are not only satisfied, they are delighted. Might they talk to their friends about you? Sure, they will! Will they send you referrals? You better believe they will. How about if you stay in touch and meet them for coffee, lunch, dinner, or invite them to a party? Instead of having a past client, you have a new friend-- and so do they. You can never have too many friends. Friends stick together, through thick and thin. They will be sending you referrals and building your pipeline. They are an unpaid and very much appreciated "sales force". How many happy past clients have become your friends? How many future clients can you turn into friends? When you get referrals from them, they have now, in a sense, become a business partner, as well. Start treating them that way. Depending on your industry, you may or may not be able to pay them for these referrals, however you can always pay them in extra time and attention. Your best friends can be your volunteer marketing team and business partners. Word of mouth marketing has always been the strongest and best conversions of business. It's a way better ROI (Return on Investment) than any form of advertising.

What do you think is easier: searching for the next deal over, and over, or having a massive volunteer army of people sending you the people they care about most? It may take more time, energy, and emotion than paying for advertising. However, I believe that growing my friend base, and in turn, growing a volunteer marketing team; is not only easier, but way more fun.

This is a mindset. How do you view your business? It can be grueling and draining, or every day can be an adventure with friends. I have been able to make my days filled with friendships and business, combined. I have fun every day and rarely consider my career work, actual work. I have been asked how many hours a day I work, and I have had trouble calculating it. Going to lunch with a friend who is also a client - is that personal friend time or is that business time? It's both. Just like hiking, walking, mountain biking, golfing, etc., with a friend who is a client. That's what will ensure that I never burn out; I get to do things I love, while conducting business. That's what keeps me passionate about what I do and how I do it. People talk about how I am always excited. Would you be excited if every day you were among friends, working with people who care about you and who are happy to see you? It's the opposite of the dreaded Monday, going to a miserable job where you don't want to see the people around you, and they may not want to see you either.

The most important first step to creating this type of sustainable business and lifestyle is to create relationships in all areas of your life that promote this success. There are so many ways you can create relationships, but remember, we are looking to create relationships that last because they know, like, and trust us. Be you, be true to who you are. You will attract those that like you for that. Be kind and considerate to others. Stick to the age-old golden rule. Treat others how you want to be treated. Smile and have a friendly disposition; that way, people will want to be around you. You get to (in essence) become a people magnet; and when you do, you will be able to build any business. It does not matter what your product is. One thing that works for me is to work on adding value to every person I encounter, each day. It doesn't matter if it's someone checking me out of a store, a waiter or waitress or someone I work with. I attempt to have a friendly disposition and engage in conversation that could add value or happiness to their day and mine.

Who Knows What You Do?

I ask again: do you attempt to separate your personal and business life? If you do, you must ask yourself, "Are you confident in what you have chosen to do/sell?" If you are passionate and confident in what you do, you will not only want people to know about

41

it, you will integrate it into most of the things you do and talk about it every day of your life. There is no separation because what you do is part of who you are. Not only will everyone in your life (currently) know what you do, everyone you meet in the future will know, too.

If you haven't made it clear to everyone in your life how you make your money, what are you waiting for? People work with people that they "know, like, and trust". Who knows you better, likes you more, and trusts you more than the people who currently choose to spend their time with you? Remember, they have choices of who they want to spend their time around, and they choose to spend it with you. Even family has choices. I am sure you know some families and some people who have chosen to stop talking to each other. If your family and friends spend time around you, they do it because they know, like, and trust you. People also have choices of who they will spend their money with or spend their money on. If they are spending money anyway on the product or service that you sell, who do you think they would rather spend it with, you or a stranger? How about you, would you prefer to spend your money in support of a friend or family member selling something you need, or would you rather put trust in a stranger and hope they don't do you wrong?

Let's put it another way. If you were going to buy a car tomorrow and you had a friend in the business would you call your friend, or would you take your chances on a stranger to not take advantage of you? I'm guessing you would rather go to someone you know. I bet you would also feel better knowing you helped your friend make money and grow their income instead of a stranger. If you bought your car from a stranger and later found out a friend sold cars, would you wish you would have known ahead of time? I bet you would, and it's the same for your people. They want to know what you do. They want to know if they need services in your industry, for which they can count on you. They would much rather see you successful, than know they helped a stranger become successful.

No matter what industry you are in, I am sure there are people in your industry (you probably know a few) that give bad service. If you don't talk to the important people in your life about your business, know that they may end up with one of the "bad" people in the business. By talking to your friends and family, you could be saving them from someone who will take advantage of them. Even if they don't need what it is that you do right now, at some point, they probably will. Do you want to find out they got taken advantage of after the fact, or do you want to save them now, before it's too late?

Not only is it important for people to know what you do, it's also important for you to stay in front of them; and continue in multiple ways to let them know you are still doing it, and that you would value their referrals. Have you ever heard, "Oh you're still doing that?" To most sales and self-employed people, that's like nails on a chalkboard. If you have systems in place that keep you and your business in front of your people, you will never hear that again.

It's easy to stay in front of people these days. It can be done through social media, cards, email, drip campaigns, newsletters, text messages, video and of course a good old-fashioned phone call or a face to face, kneecap to kneecap visit. It's important to learn about the value of automating some of this, however, not all of it. You can schedule social media posts and email and text campaigns; you can use CRMs (customer relationship management systems, that can be purchased online for a monthly or yearly fee) to easily stay in front of people. Remember, it's very easy to hide behind things like social media, emails and text messages. Any form of technology can allow you to hide. If people will continue to like and trust you, you cannot hide. You must be open and authentic. You must be accessible. So do not make all your after sale or prospective client contact automated or electronic. However, do for sure make some of it automatic with programs that you can pre-set or schedule in advance.

Chapter Five
Everyone Knows What I Do

Do you believe everyone in your life knows what you do? Are you sure they do?

What about the grocery clerk you see at the check-out line 80% of the time you buy your groceries and maybe still do not know their name? What about the owner of the dry cleaners where you drop off your clothes? How about your child's teachers? Your family doctor, dentist or the neighbor 5 doors down? Do they all know what you do, even if they, too, do not know your name? Maybe it's time to get to know their name, so that they will want to know yours.

Often, people tell me that everyone they know already knows what they do; and inevitably, as I begin to ask the questions, I come to someone that doesn't know. You have way more people in your life than you realize. You may not know all their names, but you know them, you know they exist, you engage with them and they know you, even if they don't currently know your name.

Make it Personal

I want you to take a challenge—below is a list. I want you to set a timer for 3 minutes. Read the column and then push start. As fast as you can I want you to list all the names, (or brief description if you don't know their name), that you can think of for the people in the category. When your 3 minutes are up, go to the next column and start again. This entire activity will only take you 15 minutes and I am willing to bet you can come with lots of people that you need to talk to. If you would like a bigger challenge, go to www.elliciaromo.com and download the memory jogger for a more complete list.

> School Teachers: Current and Past
> Family Doctors
> Parents of Kids in Extracurricular Activities
> Coaches
> Child Care
> Recreational Leagues
> Grocery Store
> Dry Cleaner
> Church
> Bank
> Accountant
> School Counselor
> Mechanic
> Lawyers
> Hairdresser
> Pharmacist
> People in Clubs

Former Co-workers
Former Classmates
Restaurant Servers

Okay, I've Got a List, Now What?

I bet you are now wondering how to reach out to these people. What can you say? You've never talked to them before about your work, or maybe it's been a very long time.

One of my favorites for people I haven't spoken to in a while is, "I am updating my database for my _____ business and I wanted to make sure I still had accurate contact information for you." Once you check (or get) the info, if you haven't been doing an email campaign or a newsletter to drip on them, I would ask if it is ok to add them to the email, newsletter or mailing list. Explain the values of what you send.

"Great Jane, thanks for updating your info with me. Hey, listen, I have started sending emails/newsletters to my clients about what's happening in the market (or whatever works for your business). Would it be ok if I add you to my list and send you valuable information from time to time? Perfect, thanks! I look forward to seeing you soon. By the way, who do you know that is in the market for_____?"

This can create a great lead for you, but something that is important is that you know how to ask the questions. It's not just about asking "Do you know anyone". That's a question that creates a block for the recipient. Right away people know this is a yes or no question. Put on the spot, makes it hard to think fast, it's much easier to just say no and not come up with anyone. The typical answer you're likely to hear, "Sorry, no I don't". However, if you approach it with the question posed a slightly different way, "Who do you know that is like you and would benefit from _____", or "Who do you know that I should know that needs /is looking for _____" you'd be amazed at the response you'll receive. People think about the relationships they have, they think about their friends before you even finish your question. As you can see, the way you ask your questions can make all the difference. The slight tweak of, "who do you know" rather than "Do you know anyone" can make a huge difference.

For the people whose names you didn't know, it can feel a bit more awkward. Although, it doesn't have to. You can decide: will it be easy, or will it be hard? Whatever you decide; you will be right. The next time that you are in their presence and talking to them you can simply ask, "If you had someone asking you who you know in lending, real estate, insurance (or insert your business here), do you have someone you would refer them to?" If they say no, ask them if they wouldn't mind referring people to you. If they say yes, offer them your business card. Now they know what you do, and you didn't directly ask for their business. It's casual, in conversation, and gets the point across easily. Best case scenario they say, "I have that need," and now, that person becomes a new client. Either in that moment, or the next time you see them, you can add, "Oh, by the way, I send out a monthly newsletter (or whatever works for your marketing), can I add you into my database? It's a super easy way to get their contact information, and not awkward at all, (unless you make it awkward). Make sure what it is you send, or email has value, so people look forward to getting it. If they like it, they will anticipate it and may even share it or forward it to a friend. They will notice if you miss your usual deadline, and they may even ask you about it.

The foundation of your success is found in building relationships.

Chapter Six
How to Build Relationships

When I was in the financial services industry, I would talk to and prospect random strangers, often meeting them at gas stations, grocery stores, coffee shops-- anywhere I could find people in public. I was suave enough to get them to give me their phone number. Then, I would call them up the next day and ask for an appointment in my office. I would give them the address and tell them I wanted to interview them to work with me. I had a great line (thanks to my mentors), "Are you open to new opportunities, or are you locked into your current job forever"? Do you think that was warm and inviting or does that sound strange? Most people thought it was strange. Who wants to go meet a perfect stranger who approached them in public about an opportunity to make money when they know nothing about each other? Plus, how many people get excited about going to an office? Not many I know. What I have found is things work much better, and are way easier, when you take some the time to get to know people. When I didn't know people and they didn't know me, they didn't trust me. They would set appointments with me because that line was so awesome and intriguing. Plus, who wants to say they are locked in forever? Not very many people want to say that. It makes them feel stuck.

Although they set the appointment, a huge percentage of people would not show up. They didn't respect my time because they didn't yet respect me. Once I started to build relationships first, people trusted and respected me. My no-show appointments became less and less. Now, I hardly ever have people not show up. They at least contact me to reschedule and usually will tell me why.

One great way I have found to create these connections, outside of networking events (not meeting strangers on the street) is by volunteering. What's the connection you ask? If you find an organization that you want to be involved in, then you're following a passion of your own, right? The other volunteers are following the same passion. You're working with like-minded people who have similar passions. While you're with these people, there will be small talk, simple conversations. In this situation and many others, I use an acronym, something called NEADS. This is exactly how you can craft an introduction to a relationship with those you speak to. It will work when networking, at a first meeting, at a social function, and even when volunteering.

N- Learn all about them and what is happening in their lives NOW. What do they do for work, learn about their family, how long they have lived in the area, etc...

E- What do they ENJOY? Recreational activities, about their work, about the community, if volunteering why is this organization important to them, etc…

A- What would they ALTER or change about their business, where they live, their relationships, get their goals and their pain points, etc…

D- Who are the DECISION makers? If you were going to decide to do something differently would you decide that on your own or would you make that decision together with someone?

S- Find a SOLUTION for them!

In the conversation, I will be asking questions about their lives now, what they enjoy, what they love, what brings them to the area, what brings them to this organization; and then asking them whether or not they would alter or change anything about their lives or relationships in business, etc. I ask about their goals and what is important to them. Once I've gotten this information, I decide if they are the type of person that I would like to stay in connection with. If they are, I collect their contact information. I am a card collector, not a card giver. Meaning that, I only give my card when I am asked for it. That way I can follow up to set an appointment for a one-on-one meeting to see if we would be a good match for working together, whether as a client or a potential referral partner; and of course, I am also deciding if I want them in my inner circle of friends. In this way, again, you're connecting with people who have similar passions, so you're building friendships or choosing not to. You decide if they are right for you. Just like you don't have to be friends with everyone, you don't have to work with everyone either. As my Grandmother used to say, "There are plenty of fish in the sea." It's important to remember that people want to work with those that they Know, Like, and Trust. I don't get to the D or the S in social situations. I save that for the one-on-one meeting, and then we establish whether the partnership is going to work and find out how I would be able to support them in the relationship as well. The Alter and Enjoy questions really open what I can do to add value to them. My coaching program goes more in depth with this concept, and it truly is key to building relationships that will last and will solicit more business. To learn more about working with me, directly go to www.elliciaromo.com

Aside from past clients and volunteering, how do I find these people of like mind? I go to places, classes, and events that interest me. I find people with similar interests, such as the personal growth arena, business classes (I seek out the people that are there by choice, rather than required to be there by an employer), networking groups that are more informal in nature. I have found business in a hiking group and at business happy hour mixers. There are all sorts of places and ways to find people to work with, sell to, and work alongside of. It's time to realize that almost everything you do that includes people can become your networking event. Although shopping or pumping gas can be a networking opportunity, going into the store just to find someone to talk to for business wasn't productive for me.

Once you've found people to connect with, the next step is introducing the WIFM, (What's In It For Me), concept. When it comes to working with referral partners, more often than not, the WIFM they are often looking for is a way to grow their business and have greater success. So, demonstrate in a conversation (not a monologue), how working with you will help them retain or obtain more of what they ENJOY. Find the problem and create a solution. Find a need and fill it. Help them ALTER or change things to get the results that they desire. Then you are showing them the WIFM!

What's in it for me? (WIFM) That's the magic question in everyone's head. You've started the conversation, and you've found interested parties, but the burning question is circling the air. What's in it for the potential client or referral partner? Let's face it, you have the same question when meeting people and evaluating if you want them in your life or business. You should. It's not just about what you can do for them. What need will they fill of yours is just as important. We want to create win/win situations and relationships.

When you meet with a referral partner or a client for the first time what do you focus the conversation on? Many people focus on how good they are. They want to prove the client should work with them because they are the best. That is ego centered conversation and typically it's not even a conversation, it is a monologue. This results in the client listening to you go on and on about what you can do or what you have done with your career.

The person on the opposite side of the monologue does not want to know what you have done in the past. They do not want to hear how you are the best and that you can do what others can't. What they want to learn from the conversation is how, specifically, you can help them. What, specifically, you will do for their business, their finances, or their life; if they work with you. The best way to show them WIFM (what's in it for me) is by asking them questions. Find out what they really want, using the NEADS concept. The answers will tell you exactly what they are looking for, if you ask the right questions. Then, you can offer the solution, and in doing so, give them the WIFM answer. People often want and need to feel heard. If you are guiding the conversation by asking questions; and then, actually stopping to actively listen to their answers; they will feel like they made a new best friend. Someone who was actually willing to listen and allow them to feel heard. That is a rarity in most people's lives, and they crave that.

Recently, I was coaching a loan originator. He wanted support with going into a meeting with a potential Realtor referral partner. The first thing he said to me was, "I know I have to sell the products," I instantly stopped him. Then, talked to him about going through NEADS (Now, Enjoy, Alter or change, Decision maker and Solution). I directed him to not even talk about products, unless it came up naturally through the NEADS conversation. At first, he thought I was crazy, telling him not to sell the product. I told him it's not about the product, it's about the relationship you build. Get to know the person, build rapport, see what they're about, learn what's important to them, and let them get to know you. How people feel while they are around you will always be more important than any product you are selling. He reluctantly took my advice. A few days later, after his appointment with the potential referral partner, I received an exciting text message. "I used the NEADS method at my meeting. Never talked about a program we have, and she pledged her referral business to me. All I did was talk about her life and her business. Thank you for the training."

People don't care about how much you know, until they know how much you care.

It's not about you, it's about them.

Chapter Seven

How Do I Connect?

How do people know you care? Usually from feeling heard when they talk about themselves. Most people's favorite topic is themselves. If they get to talk about themselves and you listen, they will walk away content, happy, and feeling connected to you.

My PFS (Primerica Financial Services) mentors, Garron Bond and Kevin Zirk often said, "The quality of your questions determines the quality of your results." I have since learned how true it is. If you want people to talk about themselves, you must ask the right questions about their life. What do they do for work? Why do they do it? How long have they been doing it? What keeps them in that field? What are some things they enjoy outside of work? If they could do anything differently, what would it be? The more I ask, the more they tell. The more they tell, the more they feel connected; and they will always tell me how I can fill their needs. Sales and business are often about finding the need and filling it. I have even created clients by filling a need unrelated to my product. One particular incident I recall is: a man I was prospecting needed a connection to a lawyer, and I knew someone that could be the person they needed. Once I made the connection of the two people, the person with the need bought from me, when he needed my product.

It's not always about right now either, it's often about the future. It's also not always about the person you are talking to, it's about who they know. As that guy learned of people needing my services, he referred them to me and continued to do so, because I helped him make great connections. As you may have heard, "What goes around, comes around." Help others, and they will help you; especially if they know what you want or need.

The next step? Ask them to coffee or for a one-on-one meeting to get to know each other better and find out what you can do for each other. You'll be able to decide if the relationship feels right to you, and you will then get the chance to ask for support for your business (creating referral partnerships) and/or ask for their personal business as well. Creating a new client and a referral partner. The best of both worlds. I recommend you always be thinking in the realm of "and," instead of thinking it must be either one or the other.

Wouldn't you agree that meeting for coffee, either in a breakfast restaurant or a coffee shop, with someone that you are friendly with is way more inviting than meeting in a stuffy office with someone you met for about 2 minutes, while shopping or pumping gas? Again, at this point in my career, I have set myself up for hardly any missed appointments. I make them warm, friendly and inviting and I have built rapport before asking for the meeting. I am glad that I have been able to learn from what didn't work. How often are you evaluating your activities? Are you doing the same thing over, and over again, expecting a different result? That's the definition of insanity. If you don't want to be insane, evaluate and tweak, always looking for what works and what isn't working. Constant improvement is possible.

Maybe you're asking yourself, "What does she really know? How does she know this will work for me?" or "That sounds great for you, but it's different for me." Well, I'll tell you. I started working for a mortgage company in 2013. When I started in real estate 4 years before that, as I mentioned earlier, I was flat broke and I knew no one in the industry. After working in the industry, building relationships, and using the sales foundation that I learned from my PFS mentors, I created a huge network and I generated an ongoing, sustainable business. I continue to grow my income, my business, and my friendships. I was working full time with people that I absolutely love, as the director of marketing and business development for a successful mortgage company and I have my own coaching and training business. Not only was I seeing my own success skyrocket, but I was also teaching and coaching the loan originators and Realtors that we work with, on how to increase their amount of closed purchase loans. Their success became my success, and honestly that is so thrilling to me. I love making a difference and helping others succeed. Growing and succeeding with others is way more fun than growing alone.

Without an increase in loan originators, in the first 4 years, I guided our team into closing more than 400% more purchase loans over where we were when I was hired. This isn't a coincidence. This is a proven method that has amazing results, and that's what my training classes, workshops, and book are here to do. I'm here to share my systems and methods. Nothing is a secret, and nothing is new news. I have not created a new wheel. I have listened to others, observed others and grown from others who have had success before me. I have also learned that many successful people are open to teaching and sharing with others about what made them successful. They take pride in sharing success. Life is not a pyramid, where there is only room for one at the top. Life is abundant; and we can all have success when we work with others, solve problems, and treat each other well. It's that age-old golden rule, "Treat others as you want to be treated", or "Do unto others as you would have done unto you". If you read or believe in the Judeo/Christian bible this goes with Luke 6:38. Personally, I love and appreciate those that have supported my success and helped me to grow. Therefore, if I am going to treat others as I want to be treated, I will share my knowledge, my experiences, and do the best I can to support those around me in their own success. It is just as exciting for me to be a part of your success, as it is to be a part of my own success.

There have been title and escrow professionals, insurance sales professionals, and financial service professionals that have all allowed me to coach them with tremendous success and growth in their business and their income. Some have become the heroes of their companies, being the top sales reps. If it works for me and others around me, it will work for you, too. I will and show you how to grow exponentially, in your success! You just need to do the work, follow the system, and make it happen. This book can be entertainment for you, or this book and my systems/coaching can change your business career. I am open to private and group coaching. Just go to my website for more information and for some freebies, www.elliciaromo.com

"Find something you love to do, and you'll never work a day in your life"-Harvey MacKay

That may be true, however, what if you like what you do but maybe you don't love it? Does that mean you should hurry, and find your passion doing something else? Do you ever wonder what your passion is? There are plenty of people in the world who never have an answer for 'what is their work/career passion'. There are also plenty of people in the world who believe their passion is their friends and family. People often think, I can't make money with my passion, when I am only passionate about the people I care about. How do you make a career out of friends and family?

You make your referral partners and clients your friends. You make your family and current friends your newest customers and referral partners. You create a business of fun and passion, by surrounding yourself with people that you want to be around. You can also do the things you love to do with them and make money doing it. When your friends and family are your business partners, customers, and clients you will LOVE what you do. Especially if what you are doing is making a difference in their lives. You will never dread another Monday. You will not want to watch TV, rather than work. You might even realize that TV is A.I.R (Automatic Income Reducer). You will be making a difference in the lives of people you care about, while you are working. Would this give your work more meaning? Would this enrich your life and your friends' and family's lives? Can you turn your work, business, or career into a passion? Of course, you can. It's all in the way you think about it. It's the mindset and belief that you take with you every day; every moment, and on every appointment. Be passionate about making a difference; and know that whatever product or service that you are selling is just your tool to make a difference in the lives of the people in your life. If it didn't make a difference, they would not buy from you or pay you for your service. The fact that you have customers and clients is evidence that you helped someone with something.

Building relationships with people is of the utmost importance. No one ever said on their deathbed, "I wish I worked more" or "I wish I sold more." However, they often talk about the people in their life, the relationships they've had and the experiences they had with those people. If you are working and doing business with people that you want a relationship/friendship with, you are creating experiences through your work. I often invite my work partners to do things with me that I enjoy doing. I invite them to invite their friends. We may hike together or spend an evening doing a paint class, drinking wine together. I invite them over to my house for parties. What are your hobbies and things you love to do? Can you do them with clients and referral partners? Do you mountain bike or shoot guns? How about crafts, scrapbooking, or card making? How about annual vision boards? Whatever it is that you like to do, you can do it with clients and referral partners. I promise you, these interactions will grow your business. Mix the fun times with work conversations when it comes up. I don't sell at the event, but I may create many conversations that require follow up and that's where the business closes. It's all in the follow up.

In being casual or more social about your first encounter with people, you are inadvertently saying that we can each have an evaluation period and if nothing else we have gotten to know each other better and maybe have a new friend. It's not often that I leave those interactions without feeling closer to the person. Even if it doesn't work to become referral partners or clients of each other, I usually have someone that I can be friendly with when I see them out or at a networking event. I can stay connected on social media and truly have a new friend in my life. I believe one can never have too many friends. In business, often timing is everything. It may not be the right time now, and if you don't burn the bridge, the time may be right, at some point in the future. If I am staying top of mind by staying connected, when the time is right, they may just reach out to me. Periodically, I will also check in and ask about business again. If you stop asking you may never get it. My mom always taught me to ask for what I want, so I do. I was also taught by business mentors to keep asking until they buy, die or clearly tell me to stop asking. 'No' doesn't usually mean 'no forever'. It typically means 'no for now', or 'I need more information'. If you stay persistent, they will usually come around. I have had people that I was connected to for 5 years or more that now work with me. They tell others that I was the most persistent person; always coming back to ask for the business. Now, they are so happy that I did that.

I have also experienced that it's not always about who I know, it's often about who they know. Which goes back to the value of the referral partnership, even if they are not a direct customer.

Chapter Eight
Referral Partners Are Our Friends!

If someone is referring business to you and you do not already see them as a friend, open your eyes. They most likely already consider you a friend, at least on some level. How do you make your referral partners your friends? Honestly, the bigger question is how you make friends become referral partners or how do you make a new contact, a friend and referral partner. Again, there is the age old saying that people do business with people they know, like, and trust. This comes, first! Which means a form of a friendship will also come first. They will not refer people to you, if they do not like and trust you. Turning a referral partner into a friend is kind of backwards, although not impossible either.

So, what is the first step in deepening those relationships? Again, you invite them to spend time with you. While you are together, ask them about themselves, go through NEADS, send them a card with a personal note afterward, set a second meeting time, connect on social media, learn about their life, and let them learn about yours. If you have ever said 'I don't need to make clients my friend, I just need to handle their business and do a good job,' then you are just like a loan originator who has said 'I am only as good as the last loan I've closed,' in the eyes of a realtor. Those loan originators could not be more wrong. There is a big difference in closing a transaction and burning through business just to be out looking for the next deal, and building a sustainable business which brings you referrals. Some people call it being transactional vs relational. I believe that being all about the transaction is a burn and churn method, which causes burn out, vs building a business and a life worth living, surrounded by friends and loved ones.

It's easy to quit on someone who made a mistake in a transaction or who just closed a transaction. It's easy to be swayed to work with someone else when there was no real connection. It's very easy to never send someone a business referral. It's easy to not think of you again while caught up in their busy lives. It is NOT easy to walk away from a friend. Friends stick around, friends forgive each other, and friends know that everything is not always smooth and perfect. Friends care. Friends want the best for each other. When your clients and referral partners are friends, they will refer other friends to you. They will also forgive periodic mistakes, as long as you own it, and have a plan to carry out a solution. If you don't have the solution, own that, too; and be prepared to brainstorm for one, letting them know you will share the solution with them, as soon as you have it. Be open to asking others for help, in finding the solution. Reach out to people you trust and care about. Nothing spectacular was ever done 100% by one person alone. There was always a team, coach, mentors and/or a support system, in the background.

Sometimes, I find that the person I am meeting/having coffee with already has a favorite person in the industry that I am in, and I may ask to be the best number two. I feel no shame in having a friendship and waiting in line, until the day that something may happen with the number one relationship. That person may move, leave the industry, change companies, which can create an issue; or they may have a falling out with their relationship. If we are still friends at the time that something happens with their number one person, then I will be on the top of their mind; and now the timing is right for us to do business together.

Chapter Nine
Finding Your Partners

Oftentimes when people in business think of the word partner, they think financially partnered or a team with shared commission, etc. To partner literally means "a person who takes part in some activity in common with another person(s)" Therefore, it's not as complicated as it seems.

I like to think of anyone who may send me a referral, as a partner or a friend, and I treat them as such. When I treat people as a friend and a partner, they continue to send me business. I see my referral partners as my sales force, and I don't have to pay them with a piece of the financial profit. When they bring me referrals, often they just want to be acknowledged and thanked. I like to thank people with one of the biggest and best gifts I can, my time. When we spend time together, we strengthen our relationship and often it makes our partnership in business stronger too. Of course, it's always great when you can reciprocate and give business back to them, too. Always be on alert so that you can send business their way. There are many times when someone has not sent me a referral, and I send one their way. After that, the next person they come into contact with who needs what I do, they will usually think of me first. People like to reciprocate. Most people will not want to just be a taker, receiving your referral and not returning something back to you. Even if this person doesn't see themselves as my business partner, I do look at them in this way. They may think they are "just" a friend.

At this point, you may be wondering, "Where am I going to find and grow new partnerships?" First, I would say again, drill deep into your current sphere of influence, your warm market before looking to add new people. Have you asked everyone you know (as mentioned earlier in the timed list, you can also go to www.elliciaromo.com for a more complete list) if they would refer business to you if they had the chance? If they said yes, have you discussed with them how you want to be referred? Most people in your life will want to help you, they just might not know how to. Give them a quick talk on how to refer you. I often ask them to ask their people if it's okay to give me their contact information, so that I may call them. I explain that they might be uncomfortable calling a stranger and if I call them, I can take the discomfort away. Now, they know that I want their friend's information and I don't want to hear, 'oh, I gave your card to my friend'. We all know where that leads... most of the time it leads us on the road to nowhere.

I have learned that I work best with people of like mind; and past clients that I established a positive relationship with are usually a perfect match. People in related industries are easy to create partnerships with. Often, you are going after the same target market. For instance, a title and escrow representative, a home warranty representative, and a loan originator all have a target market of Realtors, so they make perfect partners. Insurance agents who sell property casualty may want loan originators and car salespeople as partners. What industry compliments yours and would be great to establish partnerships with? How many people do you know in that industry? Where do they hang out? Do what it takes to meet those people and create friendships with them. I have a saying, go fishing where the fish are. Meaning what fish (industry professionals) do you want to catch (work with). You would not fish at a pond without fish in it, would you? So why would you go network at events that are not filled with people in your target market? Many industries have professional associations, and those associations have events and meetings. I recommend joining the associations of the industries that would make great partnerships for you and attending their events. Learn more about what they do, and meet more people in that industry. For example, if you want to meet Realtors, join the local Realtor association. If you are a property casualty insurance salesperson, you can meet loan originators at the mortgage lenders association. If you want to meet financial planners join the financial planners association, etc...

It is also important to know who your target market is. You must start with the end in mind. What do you want to create, through the people you are going to meet? This can even be done on social media, without ever leaving your home or office. Find them, and send connection or friend requests. Follow them, like their business pages, private message them and engage. After a period of time of engaging on social media, it is perfectly ok to ask for an in-person meeting. Some of my best business connections have come through an initial social media connection.

Have you ever started working with someone and wanted to quit or to fire them as a client? If you've been selling your services for more than 6 months, you have probably already experienced this. I have found that when I work with people I like; I can almost eliminate those experiences. People usually hang out with other people like themselves, therefore referrals from them create more people that I would get along well with. I have also found that when I am my authentic self, I attract the right people who want to be around me as well. Never be afraid to let your true self shine. This includes posting on your social media as well. Let your posts truly represent who you are. You will attract the people that want to be around you and the people that you want to be around. Live stream video is a great way to let your true self shine through.

When I started in the life insurance industry, I was told to talk to every adult. I was told to create partnerships wherever I go. I was challenged to talk to 10 people a day. I accepted that challenge and would not go home until I accomplished that. However, as I said before, I was asking people at the gas station, shopping centers, and at grocery stores to work with me. Oftentimes, people would look at me like I was crazy. If I got their contact information, I would follow up the next day. I learned to be good at setting appointments on the phone, so I would usually get the appointment; although, very often, as mentioned before they would not show up. I never knew why, and I was told that people were just flaky. The truth is that talking to 10 people a day about my business was a great concept. I had a poor execution of the concept. Again, when I set appointments now, I hardly ever experience people not showing up. What's the difference? It's finding the right people for me. It is also (as I stated earlier) the relationship and connections I create begin before the appointment is set up. Today, people are already pre-enrolled to work with me based on how we connected when we met.

Instead of going to gas stations and stopping random people while they are pumping their gas, I am going to events with like-minded people, or as stated previously, I am connecting through social media. Some are business networking events, some are organizations and clubs that I belong to, and some come from classes or workshops that I take for my businesses and personal growth. I find people that I can align with people who like the things I like and who have spent time in circles of people with common ground. I also find people through friends of friends (past and current clients). I ask people I respect who they know that I should know. I ask for future referrals. I remind people that I only work by referral.

Again, people are going to do business with people they know, like, and trust. When I was stopping people when they were just out and about, I didn't give them a chance to get to know me in order to decide if they would like or trust me. Therefore, it was probably weird to them that I even asked for their number and later called for an appointment for business or an interview for work. And I wondered why they didn't show up. Now it's a no-brainer to me why they didn't want to talk to me or thought I was strange. Now, instead of finding strangers and jumping into expecting an appointment for business, I build relationships and friendships. It may take longer, however, it is well worth the steps to take. I am choosing people I like, instead of talking to just anyone, and they are choosing me in return. There is mutual respect. We have both made our choices. I don't have to work with everyone and of course no one has to work with me. I have more friends, and my business is sustainable. Business comes to me, and I don't always have to seek new business. Which would you prefer, to always be out chasing the next deal, or to have business come to you?

Chapter Ten
Collaboration VS Competition

When I talk about referral partners, I do not just mean people that you can get business from. I mean a true partnership. One where each person gets and gives value. I have attended multiple conferences with VAREP (Veterans Association of Real Estate Professionals). I have been able to witness an amazing display of collaboration and partnerships at each one. This collaboration of many lenders, banks and bankers, Realtors, and veterans organizations has created some very powerful results like (at the time of this writing) 38 mortgage free homes given to deserving vets to date, over 5,000 vets supported through housing summits, and more; all in just 9 short years since the inception of the group. Results, which I believe would not have ever happened without the collaborative efforts of people that may often be competitors, rather than partners. Who are your collaborative partners? Can you turn a competitor into a partner? If so, what results do you want to be creating through those partnerships? From this group of VAREP members, I have also created business for myself. That is not my primary purpose of being at the conference and a part of the group. The primary goal is to learn and make the world a better place for our veterans. However, it is a by-product of working around people of like mind. I have given and received referral business from people across the country who knew someone that needed what I could offer where I was, in AZ. Some of those people offered the same things I do, in their area, and could be considered a competitor; however, they don't know my area, or maybe they were not licensed to do business in my state, so we collaborated on the business. What part do you play in the collaboration of partners or groups? Within VAREP I donate a lot of my time supporting others, and I believe what comes around, goes around. I may not always reap an equal benefit from this group to my giving; however, I believe and have experienced in my life, that my giving comes back to me tenfold, I just never know where it will come from. It doesn't have to come from the source that I gave to.

Partnerships are a no-brainer, know that you absolutely need them. Think of every super successful person you know. Did they do it 100% on their own? Chances are, they did not. They had mentors, coaches, and partnerships. Partners come in many forms. Partners will build your pipeline, and you should be finding ways to give to their business, as well. The easiest way to do this is to co-brand your marketing. Share in marketing efforts and costs. The most valuable is to build relationships and do the things together that will build each of you up. Being a part of a mortgage company, we align our brand with the brand of Realtors and Real Estate Companies often. In order to be sure that we are aligned to create a mutually beneficial partnership, we must have great communication and discussions, before we start to market our alignment together. We make sure we are like minded. We create a co-branded marketing plans together. You can co-brand anything, print, on-line, or live events; with other professionals in related fields. Who will you consider co-branding and partnering with? I am sure by now, you have someone in mind. Challenge yourself and reach out to them within 24 hours of reading this, and ask for an appointment to discuss the opportunity.

My suggestion is to find a professional that you love and respect, and is in a related industry. An industry that can complement yours or an industry that has the same target market as you do. Partner with them in sponsoring classes or events. Show yourself as partners in the industry by sharing connections and referrals. Just like Mike Kortas (founder and CEO of NXA mortgage) and I did when we first met, as I mentioned in the beginning of the book. I recommend partnering together to create events to network with each other's sphere of influence. Bringing your people and their people together at an event will allow you the opportunity to physically introduce them to your people, and you get to be introduced to their people. There is nothing better than face-to-face introductions, when you are dealing with a service-related business. A great way to do this is a business mixer either at a local bar, restaurant, your office, a club house, or even in your home. I also love doing educational workshops. What is a topic in your industries that people often have questions about? Answer the most asked questions in a workshop, and discuss how your industries work together and why you chose to partner with each other. You each get a chance to help build the other's credibility to the audience.

I recommend partnering together to create events that allow you to network with each other's sphere of influence. It gives your business professional connections a chance to network with their business professional contacts, and vice versa; possibly creating even more opportunities than you could ever dream of. When your people grow as a direct result of something you did for them, they will always remember that. Look for ways to help the partner succeed, even when it doesn't directly benefit you. For example, intentionally creating those moments of introductions for others to meet. It's not just about who you meet, it's also about who you can connect together. Be sure to provide recommendations and testimonials, either in person, in writing, or in a video. This will not only help their reputation; it also illustrates your generous spirit, while promoting the partnership. Neither party should be just a giver or just a receiver. You all can collaborate to create an amazing network of people. You can have classes, do an open house, customer appreciation event, or a simple happy hour. As you build relationships, you will grow your business. As I have said before, people do business with people they know, like, and trust. The more you do together and the more you do for your partners, the more they will like you and trust you. You can co-brand any of these events with these people. Use the marketing of the event as a co-branding opportunity. That way, even if there are people that cannot attend, they see the partnership and it starts the branding. Whether or not they attend, people from the other person's sphere will begin to see and know your brand and your people will see theirs. Again, this is a win-win opportunity.

You've connected, you've made relationships, and you've found partners that you want to work with. Now, you can focus on building that referral business. Are you getting referral business? Do other professionals want to send their clients to you? If the answer is yes, Congratulations!!!!

If the answer is that you struggle in this area, you may want to ask yourself: are you relevant to others, and are you asking for the business? Referral partners, friends, and family will want to give you business if they feel that you are connected to them and you can and will connect with their people. Are you asking for referrals? It's easy to think people will refer you just because they like you, however they may not think of it, if you don't ask. How many times in your life, before you were in the business world have you randomly sent business people a referral lead? Probably not too often. Most people who like you will want to help you, they just don't always know how. Ask for what you want, and most likely you will get it. It is also important to stay top of mind. Some people think asking once and being told one time, that someone will send them a referral lead if they have it, is enough. These people are not constantly thinking of you and your business. They have their own lives to lead. It is extremely important to stay in front of people. To remind them that you work by referral and to periodically ask them who they know that might need what you provide. Our technology today makes this simple. You can automate a drip campaign over email, you can use text messages and videos; and social media can keep you in front of people, literally, on a daily basis.

For many people, giving a referral brings to mind the age-old question of what's in it for them (WIFM – What's in it for Me?) and can they trust you. Sometimes, what's in it for them is just a feel-good thing because they feel you care about them and in turn, they want to help someone who cares. The referral can/may be a gift. However, would you be getting the gift, if you didn't have a meaningful relationship, first? Other times, they may want recognition. Thank you cards and a public thank you on, social media, can do wonders. Depending on your industry, you may be able to share your commission, or you can send them a gift card or flowers. You can do a referral partner appreciation event, aside from a client appreciation event. Everyone who sent you at least one referral can attend. Another great way to thank someone is to show up at their office with a thank you gift basket, plant, flowers, balloons, etc.... Now you are not only thanking them and giving them recognition for the referral, you are also opening up the opportunity to meet the people they work with. Of course, if the situation warrants it, returning the favor by sending a referral lead back to them will always be appreciated. No matter what you do, do something. People like to be recognized for their efforts. It doesn't matter if the lead pans out. Acknowledge the behavior with positive reinforcement, and the behavior is likely to be repeated. Just like when you were a kid and your teachers or your parents rewarded you for something you did, didn't you want to do it again?

Chapter Eleven

Build the Relationship, But Don't Get Burned!

In the world of real estate and mortgage I have built a sustainable business through building relationships. I get referrals often without asking for them. People call me to work with me. I have people to reach out to because their friend or colleague told them to. I also have people reaching out to me, asking me to contact someone they know that can use my help. My friends, clients, and past clients come back to me with repeat business because of our friendship. Nothing I have today is because I made a sale. Everything is because I have built relationships, friendships, and partnerships. People trust me, so they continue to stick around me. When they stick around, they see how much I care. They feel my passion, and we have fun together. My clients and partners give me business through referrals. I also give them what they're needing. The win/win scenarios created have helped me to hit many of my goals. Find a need, and fill it. Often, I go through the NEADS questions mentioned earlier to find that need. Otherwise I will just ask, "How can I support you" or simply, "What do you need"?

"You can get everything in life you want, if you will just help enough other people get what they want." Zig Ziglar

Are you a giver? Most people strive to be givers; however, it is important to receive as well when you are in a partnership. It's just like breathing, you must exhale as well as inhale. It needs to be win/win. If you are a bad receiver you are stopping someone else's giving. How do you think they would feel if they are wanting to give, and you block that by not allowing their giving to come to you? I have experienced that in my life. I have had gifts returned to me when the receiver refused to receive. I can tell you that I felt hurt. I wanted to do something that would allow the other person to feel happy, and instead I felt like a failure at giving. I am sure you don't want your people to feel like a failure at being a giver, so it's up to you to be as good at receiving as you are at giving. Imagine if you only breathed air out, giving carbon monoxide to the environment and the plants that need it. What would happen to your body, if you did not receive the oxygen that the plants produce? You would die. It's just the same in business, you must do both, give and receive, in order to be successful.

If you are always the giver, you may not be getting paid your worth. I mean this in both tangible and intangible ways, it can be through money or even just an appreciation of your efforts. The other person may just be taking advantage of you. It's just as important for you to ask for what you need (actually more important), as it is to only find out what the other person needs and to fill that need. If you don't ask, you often don't get.

I had to learn this the hard way. I was working as a marketing rep in the title and escrow business, like I mentioned before. I had heard the phrase "Givers gain and give others what they want in order to get what you want." Although that is or can be true, I learned that they also had to know what I wanted. Sometimes, I assumed they knew. Other times, they did know, but since I never specifically made my expectations clear we didn't really have a partnership. So they would take what I gave, but not necessarily give back. These moments are lose/win rather than win/win. I was allowing myself to lose because I did not value my receiving as well as I valued giving. At one point in my life I was especially ineffective at receiving. I felt awkward and guilty when I was given a gift, even if that gift was a simple compliment. I did not know how to receive, and I would deflect. I made it like it was no big deal or I would say no thank you. I was not a gracious receiver at all. If you are like me, it's easy to give, and not so easy to take or receive. I had to learn though, that in order to be successful, both are necessary. Just like air, oxygen, and carbon dioxide.

I can remember two clients, specifically. Well, actually one never became a client because I never directly asked for the business. We met, and he knew I wanted his business; although at the time he wasn't willing to give it to me. I asked him what he needed because I thought if I worked hard enough in giving him what he needed, he would eventually send me his referral business. This man was a pretty high producing realtor, and the owner of a real estate company. He was looking to build a team and get his business off the ground. He recently started a new real estate company and at that time only had a few agents. He was struggling to recruit and keep agents in his company. He was specializing in short sales at the time, and he needed a good lawyer. I was friends with the lawyer he wanted. I set up a lunch appointment, in order to introduce them. This was my way to show him that I could add value to his business. We all went to lunch and the two of them began to do business together. Then he told me about wanting to recruit agents and grow his company quickly. I knew another real estate company owner who did exactly what he wanted to do. I asked her to meet with him. I never told him that in return, I wanted some of his business. I felt like I was doing this in good faith, and that he would just return the favor. In that meeting, I acted like his secretary and took copious notes. When the meeting was over, I sent them to him. He asked me what realtors I knew that wanted to change companies. I set up an interview for him to meet one of my realtor friends. He hired him. In the end, I handed him a realtor to grow his business with, a business growth plan, and a preferred legal connection all for free. I worked hard for this man, and

I received nothing in return. Although I never set my expectation up front, I realized what I was doing, and I stopped working for free. Although in this case, my time and efforts were already taken. I gave and did not specifically ask for something to receive. I was not clear in my expectations and was uncomfortable at the time being direct in what my needs were. He may have known what I wanted, and he may not have given it because I didn't speak up. I learned my lesson the hard way. It may not always be easy to ask for what you want or need. However, it is necessary and gets easier, the more you do it. Feel the fear, and do it anyway, or you will be out of business, struggling, or riding the inevitable sales roller coaster.

Another experience started in a similar fashion and ended very differently. This time, I stopped the insanity. Once I realized that I was repeating the same actions and expecting a different result, I set up a meeting. I had what I thought was going to be a hard conversation. Scared and shaking I walked into his office and asked, are you happy with what I have done for you? Would you agree that your business has grown as a result of the meetings I have set up for you and the people I have introduced you to? He agreed that it had. Then I told him, I cannot keep working for you for free. I need you to reciprocate and pass some business back my way. "Will you open some escrows with me, so that we can continue to work together?" He didn't even realize that every time he opened an escrow, he wasn't thinking of me or my company. He was working out of old habits, and I learned the lesson of asking for what I needed. The conversation also wasn't as hard or scary as I thought it would be. When he realized what he was doing, he felt badly and wanted to make it right. Within a few days, I had multiple business deals going with him. We worked in partnership, until I left the title industry; and we are still friends, to this day.

From that day forward, when I was setting up referral partnerships, I was very clear with my expectations from the beginning. I set up my first meeting to decide if I want to work with them and allow them to assess if they want to work with me. I get to know them as a person. I still find out what they need first, and then, I will be sure to tell them what I need, as well. I ask if they are open to working together, and we can fill each other's needs. Then, if we are both on the same page with sharing business and referrals, I set a second appointment, so that we can create an actual game plan of how that will look.

Never again, will I walk away, planning to work for someone else (meaning send them business, and referrals, and meeting their needs) and being what I think is a good partner, without them also understanding my expectations of how the partnership benefits me as well. This, then, becomes a true partnership; we each give and we each receive. Now that you've got the partners, let's talk more about how you keep them and how you grow together.

Chapter Twelve
Exchange of Value

You may be able to work your sphere of influence in more ways than just exchanging business, as well. Another key point my PFS mentors, Kevin and Garron taught me: it's not always about who you know, it's often about who they know, as well. I have also learned that I cannot do it all; and the more I leverage other people's time, energy, and money, the better off my experience can be. I have come to realize that if I want to leverage others, I better be willing to allow others to leverage me, as well. Meaning, make it win/win. Create a scenario that is good for everyone. Let each person work within their core values and strengths.

A perfect example of what I am talking about was a time when I met my now good friend and owner of RE/MAX Prime in Paradise Valley, AZ; Dennis Rosvall. I was selling ads for The Real Estate Book at the time. Dennis wanted no part of buying print ads at the time. He shot me down pretty hard, telling me that he would never buy an ad. Most people in sales like to get a firm Yes or a No, rather than a maybe; so I could appreciate his firm response. Most people would also not continue to talk to him or pursue him after that. However, my philosophy is not to burn bridges and to build friendships, so I continued to talk to Dennis, just not about buying an ad.

Dennis ran a monthly Realtor home tour. Where Realtors were invited to tour homes that were for sale in the area and offer feedback to the listing agent. They looked for their buyers and networked with each other. He had expenses associated with that tour. He served breakfast and paid for a meeting space where the agents started the tour. He helped cover those expenses by offering sponsorships to people in exchange for them getting to network and promote themselves to the attendees. Because I chose to build a friendship with Dennis after he said no, when the opportunity came up for him to find a new sponsor, he offered me the ability to step in. I jumped at it. Over time, through that tour, I met many more friends and massively increased my ad sales. Many of those people are still my friends today. Many of those people who weren't ready to do business with me 10 years ago have since conducted successful business transactions with me and referred me more clients. One simple act of creating a friend out of someone that said no to my sales pitch, has helped my business and personal friendships to a level that is immeasurable. My life has had such a positive impact through getting that no. Today Deniss is one of my closest friends and we do share referrals and work together in business now. What do you do when you hear 'no'? It's your choice how that no will impact your day, your business, and your life. Do you walk away and think there was no value in meeting that person, or do you keep them in your database and on your social media? Do you stay in touch or do you never speak to them again?

When I worked for the title company, I had an insurance agent as a friend on Facebook. We met face-to-face, at a vendor expo event. He was talking to a mutual friend. When he was introduced to me, I told him we were friends on Facebook. He thought about who I was, then said, "You're an account executive for title, right"? I confirmed, and he went on to tell me that I was of no use to him because he had never received a referral from a title rep before. Did I want to stay in contact with him after that? Of course not. About a year later, I started working for Peoples Mortgage Company as the Director of Marketing and Business Development. Guess where many property casualty insurance agents like to get their referral business...from lenders. Loan Originators are often the most beneficial business relationships to these insurance agents. Now guess who wanted to reconnect with me, so that he can meet the loan originators at Peoples. This same guy. Did I want to spend time with him now, when he dismissed me before? Of course not. The lesson here is to be careful how you treat people, and know that it isn't only about the person you are talking to now. It's also about who they know, now and who they will know, in the future. It's about building a relationship and a connection and treating people well, no matter if they will add value to your business right now or not. At some point they probably will add that value, as long as you treat them with respect. Be the person that others want to be around, it will pay off. Do what it takes to become a people magnet, and draw them to you.

What are ways you can trade value or trade connections, in your industry? Think outside the box. I'll use my friend Ryan, who is a CPA, as an example. When you think about real estate or lending, would you think CPA? Of course not. However, Ryan and I trade value because business people need to know about how to structure their taxes. I periodically gather my clients and other business referral partners and have Ryan educate them on tax laws and information that they need to know. Ryan offers them a discount if they use his services, because they came through our partnership. Everyone wins. My clients get the knowledge they need, I have a few minutes in front of them and I tell them if they find value in his talk I would appreciate it if they show me by sending me their next referral. Of course, I know they will get value, so I will get referrals. It is super important for me to stay top of mind and having my people face-to-face, in front of me, is the best way to stay top of mind. Plus, I am in front of at least 10-15 people at once. How long would it take me to meet with those 10-15 people, all individually? Ryan gets new clients, and my people get an amazing connection to a great CPA. There is no way to lose, with an exchange of value like this. Who do you know that has information that others will want? You may want to ask them to teach a class for you and your people.

I do this with many other professionals, in multiple other industries, as well. I have an estate planner that has talked to my clients about the importance of trusts. I have had an interior designer talk about decorating, a financial planner talk about retirement accounts, an HOA manager talk about how to work with your HOA and get results, etc....

What ways can you help your partners meet your people that will help everyone involved? It can be a simple networking happy hour or client's appreciation event or a class such as these. If nothing else, you can always advertise together, saving money and targeting the same people. You can create newsletters together so that your info gets to their database, and vice versa. If you come up with something creative and new, please share your ideas. Sharing ideas is a great way of giving. Know that others can use the idea, and it will not diminish the amount of business you can get. There are enough people on this planet for us all to have plenty of business and enough wealth to be spread around. I have learned that when I share my ideas of what has worked, many people won't do it, anyway. It's easier for people to stay in the status quo, than to make changes. Even if the status quo is not where they want to be. Humans are lazy, and change takes effort. I would love to hear your success stories, whether it was from taking my advice or an idea that came to you through reading this. Please email me at elliciaromo@gmail.com

Chapter Thirteen

Getting and Keeping Loyal Partners

You have the foundation, you're partnered, and you're getting referrals. How do you build and maintain loyalty? You have read about building relationships, friendships and creating business partners. In my opinion, building the relationship, builds the loyalty. It's easy to quit on someone who did a transaction for you or with you, did your taxes, sold you a plan or program or an insurance policy, etc... It's hard to quit on a friend. Friends stick together. Friendship adds a human element. Friends want the best for each other; and when necessary, friends accept and forgive human errors. It's not about the mistake made, it's about how you handle it. When things are going well, you don't ever have to worry about losing partners. It's when something goes wrong that we worry. It's the friendship that will make the business survive the rough spots. Be the example of what you want. When there is a problem, most people respect the person who owns up to it and talks about how they are working on fixing it. Most people get annoyed by the person who makes excuses. I recommend that you think of potential solutions, then own the problem; allowing the other person time to adjust and hear your potential solutions. Do not give excuses, reasons, or justifications. That just upsets people more; and most of the time, people do not care why something happened. They just care about the end result and what will happen to them. If it's a problem, they want to know if you will fix it, and not why the problem happened, in the first place. If they are upset, hear them out; and then thank them for making you aware of how they feel. Getting defensive and justifying your position will get you nowhere.

The other thing is making sure you are also loyal to your people. You cannot expect them to be loyal if you are not also loyal. You do not attract what you want, you attract what you are. How do you treat them when they make mistakes? Do you threaten to leave the partnership, or are you calm and understanding? Do you react or respond to situations? Do you repel people or are you a people magnet? Be the magnet, make it so that people want to be around you. Be the most positive person in the room, and people will come back for more. People are attracted to positive, upbeat happy people.

I recently asked a group from my group coaching program what makes them loyal to service providers that they choose to work with. I will challenge you to think about the same thing. What makes you loyal to someone is probably exactly what would make someone else loyal to you. Would you stay with someone if they just did their job or met your most basic expectations? Would it take them going above and beyond? Would it take a friendship? Would you want to know they care, and they are not just doing their job? Would you want to feel like they have your back and they will make sure you are always satisfied with their work? Will you want to know they are doing the best they can and that they are more than competent to get the job done? They want the same from you.

Some of the answers that came out in the mastermind group were:

Professionalism, getting things done in a timely manner, being treated with respect and having our time respected, having the same values, being responsive, being accessible, being truthful, having high integrity and ethics; being supportive, not just in business, but also in general life; showing they care about me as a person.

Quitting on a friend is way harder than quitting on a person you just send business to.

If your clients were your friends, would they think twice about leaving you if you made a mistake? Do friends understand when mistakes happen if you own them and do what it takes to right the wrong? Do friends give second chances? Would you or do you give your friend a second chance and be more lenient with your friends when they mess up? I bet you do.

Building relationships and taking responsibility for your actions, doing the right thing and acting as a true professional, and going above and beyond when possible will always build you loyalty. Do what you want others to do, in order to gain your loyalty.

As the Bible states, "*Do unto others as you would have them do unto you*".

The following is a testimonial to Patricia Bahr (a loan originator at Peoples Mortgage Company at the time) from one of her Realtor partners. After reading this ask yourself, do you have any question of his loyalty to her? Notice he called her a friend, and it did not start out that way:

"Let me take a moment to tell you about one of my favorite people Patricia Bahr Aranzaens. I met Patricia about 14 years ago when I had a client who wanted to buy a property and no one else seemed to be able to put it together. Patricia came to the rescue! My client was a 19 year old first time home buyer and the complex took special financing but Patricia got it done. She was so friendly and courteous while doing a wonderful job and working really hard. That business relationship has grown into a friendship and deep respect over the years. I have never had to think twice about her true care for her clients and expertise in her field. Never once in all these years have I needed to wonder if Patricia was telling the whole truth. It is truly a blessing when you find a wonderful person who is also great at their job and get to work with them for years. If you need a Realtor please consider contacting me but if you need a loan I always recommend Patricia."

Let's Connect

Do you have loyal partners? Partners like Patricia has created? If so, you may want to ask them why they stay loyal to you. Then, repeat the actions that created the current loyalty with other people in your life. When you get the results you want, repeat what you did to create that result, over, and over, and over again.

"If you go looking for a friend, you're going to find they're very scarce. If you go out to be a friend, you'll find them everywhere." Zig Ziglar

That includes the people inside of your business.

In this book, we've laid the foundation of building business, through building relationships. Stay in contact, stay in front of your people, and stay top of mind. Give and receive, be clear about what you want to create, create win/win scenarios. Find the need and fill it. Give others what they want, so that you can get what you want. Be a friend, and become a people magnet. Be loyal, so that others will be loyal back to you. Be the person, client, business partner, that you want others to be towards you. Love who you are. Love the business you're in, and love the people you surround yourself with. Do these things, and you will reap great rewards; not only in business, but also in life, in general. You will be rewarded and fulfilled with tremendously powerful connections and partnerships.

My coaching and my workshops are designed to dive deeper and help you figure out exactly what to do and say to gain the kind of success that myself and others have had, through using this process. If you want to see measurable growth, increased income, success, happiness, and most importantly, to build your business with the right kind of relationships for you; join me in my coaching program, mastermind groups, or one of my workshops! Your success is my passion.

I encourage you to keep building your friendships. Find the people that you want to work with. Find those people who can be part of your network; who can help you grow your business. It's not always who you know or who you meet, it's who they know and who they can lead you to as well. Be positive and happy—draw people to you. Support others, send business their way; and they will find ways to send some of it back to you, too. To learn more, join me at www.elliciaromo.com where you can sign up for a workshop, small group coaching, or private coaching; and we will cover these topics in further detail. Connect with me on Facebook, Instagram or LinkedIn and Subscribe to me on YouTube for my video tips. Email me at elliciaromo@gmail.com There is a lot of fun involved in appreciation of our partners. I look forward to seeing you soon, either in person working with me, or on social media. Let's connect and get to know each other. We can each be a part of building business with relationships together. I would love to see and hear about your success in building your business worth living for.